Level Up

From the Court to the Classroom to Community
(Basketball Tips and Tools for Success in Life)

Level Up

From the Court to the Classroom to Community
(Basketball Tips and Tools for Success in Life)

Sammy Clark

Copyright © 2021 Sammy Clark. All rights reserved.

This book or any portion thereof may not be reproduced or used in any manner whatsoever without the publisher or Sammy Clark's express written permission except for the use of brief quotations in a book review.

Printed in the United States of America

First Printing, 2021

ISBN: 978-1-951883-46-1

Photos and interviews used with permission.

The Butterfly Typeface Publishing
PO Box 56193
Little Rock AR 72215

Dedication

In loving memory of Charles Ripley

6/12/1946 - 6/28/2020

It All Starts Right Here.

LEVEL UP!

Table of Contents

Take the Shot	1
Chapter 1: Focus Points	12
Determine Your Why	15
Chapter 2: Focus Points	17
The Coaches' Zone	21
Coach Ramona McGee	22
Coach Marcus D. Davis	25
Coach Ray Barefield	28
Coach Antonio Buchanan	31
Coach Daryl Fimple	35
Coach Marland Smith	40
Coach Marlon Staton Jr. (Coach Pop)	44
Coach Brandon Taylor	49
Coach Ronnie Williford	54
Coach Johnnie Harris	59
Coach Eric Musselman	64
Coach Jermaine Johnson	68
Chapter 3: Focus Points	71
Photo Gallery	72
Tryouts	91
Chapter 4: Focus Points	93

Mental Toughness   **95**

   Chapter 5: Focus Points   100

Developing Your Skills   **105**

   Chapter 6: Focus Points   107

Game Day   **108**

The Knowledge Tree   **113**

   Whitney Jones   114
   Ryven "Trigger" Jackson   115
   AJ Walton   117
   Kim Adams Jr.   118
   Vincent Hunter Jr.   120
   Tyler Scaife   121
   Ricshanda Bickham   123
   Kameisha Johnson   125
   Taylor Mumphrey   126
   Terrell   128
   Anonymous   129
   Shekinna Stricklen   131
   Nyeshia Stevenson   132
   Nakeia Guiden   134
   Tiffany Davis   136

   Chapter 7: Focus Points   138

Building A Positive Support System   **149**

   Parents of 2020 Mc Donald's All-American   150
   Datron and MeLesha Humphrey   152
   Anonymous Parents   154
   Stacey and Yvonne Stevenson   156
   Anthony and Loretta Walton   159
   Strength Coach Whitney Jones   162

Chris Davis	166
Player Development and Skills Training	168
Chapter 8: Focus Points	170
Ranking and Playing on a National Level	**173**
Chapter 9: Focus Points	181
Set Your Table	**187**
Chapter 10: Focus Points	191
Daily Journal	**193**
About the Author	**235**

Acknowledgments

Thank you to everyone who has given their time, input, and suggestions to help me through this process. And a special thanks to Rodney Newsom and Natasha Clark for their support and countless hours along the journey.

Coach Sammy Clark

Introduction

The primary mission of Level Up is to inform and strengthen the student-athlete. Level Up seeks to engage the student-athlete in developing their understanding of the purpose of basketball and its emphasis on developing life skills. This will help the athlete make sound decisions in different environments and circumstances.

Driven by knowledge and experience, a "Level Up Mindset" can guide athletes toward improving basketball skills on the court and in life. I desire to pass on critical values that can be used for generations to come.

When I was a kid, my coach, Marcus Davis, would have us run line drills before shooting free throws and for every shot that was missed, we would have to run two extra line drills. Coach Davis would say, "Son, you're not focused! Hard work makes winners!"

Coach Davis knew the player's mind was so focused on the line drills and not the free throws that even a simple task such as a free throw required their full concentration.

Years later, I went back to visit my old school and spoke with Coach Davis about how frustrated the team would be after running and being so tired that they would miss just about every free-throw shot because of it.

The coach explained that one shot can be the difference between a win or loss and that it takes a lot of confidence and focus on blocking out the crowd, the opposing team, and getting into the correct focus zone to think about this one shot that can impact the game.

As a coach and educator, I must prepare students to change their values, help increase their understanding, and make them aware of their purpose so that when tough challenges arise—on and off the court—they have the skills and knowledge needed to tackle them.

Sports are not just about winning or losing but more about preparation (plan to succeed), understanding (know all), and Purpose (giving it your all every day).

Enjoy your process to greatness and always better your best.

Chapter 1

Take the Shot

Beginner Player vs An Advanced Player. Shows development.

Working hard to set the stage, John pushed the basketball across the court. He looked back and forth between the coach and his father, who were both on the sideline.

"Pass the ball!" the crowd shouted.

"Take the shot!" John's dad yelled.

John quickly dribbled the ball across the half-court line and the coach who had been sweating, yelling, and running up and down the side-line the entire game, yelled for him to call a time out.

"Time out!" John yelled out. He hustled to the huddle; all he could think about was what this win could mean.

The game was being played in the back gym of the Boys and Girls Club in Arkansas—the same gym where most high-school stars got their first shot at organized basketball.

John imagined being just like those high-school basketball players his dad talked about every day and took him to watch every Friday.

The time out was over and John was back on the court. He could hear his father's voice in his head.

"Make me proud, Son. Take the shot!"

The ball was inbounded to John. He crossed a player over, used a spin move on another player, and looked to take the shot. Instead, he passed the ball to his teammate, who didn't get the shot off in time.

John watched as his coach kicked over the chair.

As John walked slowly to the bench, the coach said, "John, you made the right basketball play. However, that's not what I drew up. I wanted you to take the shot."

Just then, John's dad stormed the court, and before the team could shake hands, he yelled, "John, you're not shaking hands!" He insisted. "You lost the game for your team. No ice cream after the game, and you won't be watching the high-school play on Friday!"

John's friend, Tim, lived in Texas and played at a local YMCA. Tim averaged 12 points and 6 rebounds all season. Tim's parents were not able to make any of the regular-season games.

"I promise to make it to the championship game," Tim's dad said.

Tim was motivated to win.

Friday night arrived, and Tim was energized and full of joy. Tonight's game would be the first time of the season that his dad would be in attendance to watch Tim play.

Tim played so well that his coach gave him regular-season MVP and made him co-captain for the tournament.

Game day arrived. Tim was so hyped during warm-ups. After having a great warm-up, he ran, jumped up, and touched the bottom of the net.

Tim looked into the crowd for his dad, but he was nowhere to be found.

"Play ball!" the referee said in a loud voice.

There was no time to be sad. Tim got the ball off the tip and came down, dribbling fast. A quick look at the coach told him it was too early to shoot the 3-pointer, but Tim was in motion to shoot before the coach could utter the words. His mind was made up. This shot was going down.

Afterward, Tim looked at the coach, who smiled and said in a low voice, "Good shot."

Before the ball could get across the half-court line, Tim jumped into the passing lane and stole the ball. He took two dribbles and made another 3-pointer!

"Time Out!" the other team called.

Tim ran to the bench with the other players.

"It's your night, Son!" the coach shouted.

Tim sat down for a second and looked around to see if his parents had made it.

"Have you seen my parents?" Tim asked the coach. "My dad promised he would be at the game."

"Stay focused," the coach told Tim. "Your dad will come."

Tim did as he was told and finished the tournament with an all-time high, 42 points. Tim became the first ever to score 42 points in a championship game. He also became MVP of the regular season and championship.

Tim was full of mixed emotions. He was happy his team had won, but he was sad his dad hadn't been there to see him play.

He sat with his head down.

"Tim," the coach said, "your dad texted me five minutes before the game. He said he had to work overtime. He said he needed the money to get the car fixed."

Tim nodded. He understood, but he was still disappointed.

On the ride home, the coach tried to cheer him up.

"Tell your dad how hard you played, and let him know you did a great job," the coach encouraged. "Try to stay positive."

Knowing the young boy needed cheering up, the coach added, "Hey, would you like to go with me to watch my son play? He is All-American for his high school. He has plans to play professionally after playing one year of college basketball."

Tim nodded and couldn't stop smiling the whole ride home.

When he got home, he ran into his house full of renewed joy.

"Mom. Dad. Guess what?" Tim said excitedly. "Coach is taking me to go watch an All-American play next week. He plans on going to the NBA soon, just like me."

"Slow down," Tim's dad smiled at his son's enthusiasm. "Tell me about your game."

"I did well," Tim told his parents. "I played just like Kobe Bryant. I couldn't miss a shot. My first shot was a 3-pointer, and I made it all nets."

"Great job," Tim's dad said. "I'm sorry I couldn't make it to the game. I had to work overtime."

"Coach told me," Tim said sadly. "I don't understand why. If you work all week, do you still have to work overtime too?"

"Just keep living," Tim's dad said. "One day, you will."

The Showcase Game

It was finally game day, and Tim found it hard to focus on his homework.

He had been shooting hoops outside in the park all week. He pictured himself as an All-American taking the last shot of the game and scoring to win the championship.

At 5:30 that afternoon, the coach pulled up to Tim's house.

"I'm gone," Tim yelled to his parents. "Coach Mike is here."

As he jumped into the car, he noticed that the coach's son, Mike Jr., was in the front seat.

"What's up, *lil* man?" the 6'6" point guard said to Tim. "How you doing?"

"I'm okay," Tim answered in a low voice.

"I heard about your championship game the other day," Mike Jr. said. "You scored 42 points in one game!"

Shaking in his shoes, Tim smiled and said, "Aw, it was nothing." He couldn't believe he was talking to one of the best high school players in the country.

"You must be better than me," Mike Jr. told Tim. "I only average

33 points a game."

"I guess you're right," Tim smiled. "But I have a question. Did I miss the game? Why are you already sweaty?"

"I play on a different level," Mike said. "You have to do pregame workouts if you want to play at a high level each night."

Finally, they arrived at the gymnasium. Mike Jr. got out and headed to the back door of the gym.

"Good luck," Tim yelled as he and Coach Mike walked around to the front of the gym to check in.

As they entered, the smell of popcorn took over, and Tim ran to buy some. While waiting in line, Tim noticed how many people knew Coach Mike.

People walked up to him and said things like, "What a great son you have. He could go professional tomorrow," and "I can't wait to see him at the next level."

Tim was even more shocked when a man recognized him and said, "Great game you had the other day."

After they got popcorn, the horn sounded, signaling that it was time for the game to start. Tim and Coach Mike found and took their seats. The gym was packed; there was standing room only.

The visiting team got the ball first, and Mike Jr. ran into the passing lane for a steal. Then, he shot a 3-nothing-but-net shot.

Coach Mike jumped for joy and said, "That's my boy!"

The very next play, the guard drove the ball hard to the basket, but Mike Jr. jumped high, blocked the shot, and took the ball down the court with a crossover into a slam dunk. He got fouled.

Mike Jr. made the free throw and sent the team into 40 minutes of hell ball pressure that forced the team to turn the ball over three times. Mike Jr. got up nine quick points in 40 seconds. He was focused, and there was no way the other team could beat him.

Mike Jr.'s team kept the pressure on and gained a 20-point lead by halftime.

Tim was in pure amazement of Mike Jr.

Tim saw how full of joy his coach was over his son, but he had two questions he wanted to ask.

Later, he asked, "Coach, why were you so happy when Mike Jr. shot a 3-pointer, but when I took a 3-point shot, I knew you didn't want me to take it?"

I can't believe Tim asked me that, the Coach thought to himself. *But I need to answer, so I can help him level up his way of thinking and his gameplay.*

"Mike Jr. is a senior," Coach Mike explained. "He works out three times a day and shoots 500 3-pointers, five days a week. You practice twice a week and work out only on Saturdays—if we don't have a game. Tim, I need you to understand that the chances of you taking or making a shot are low. I only want you to take the highest percentage shot first."

Coach Mike looked into Tim's eyes, and expecting him to finish his sentence, he asked, "Which is…?"

"The layup," Tim answered in a low voice.

Coach Mike went on to explain, "Everything in basketball should be done with understanding and purpose. I'm only the coach. The true result lies in the hands of the players, and you must deal with the outcome."

The horn sounded, and half-time was over. Mike Jr. was ready to hit the hardwood running. The visiting team was on a run, 20-0. The game became a back and forth race until the fourth quarter, with only 30 seconds left.

Mike Jr. had a chance to make history. He had 30 points, 10 assists, 10 rebounds, and a chance to make the game's last play. Mike Jr. brought the ball down the court, called the set out loud, "1-4 flat," and drove the ball to the free-throw line. He pulled up and missed the whole rim.

Later, as he walked to shake the other team's hand, he looked every player in the eye as he said, "Great job."

When he got to the opposing coach, the coach said, "I love how hard you play, but I respect the man you have become. Not many people can lose a valuable game and still have respect for the other team."

Looking right into the eyes of the coach, Mike Jr. said, "My dad always taught me to level up, show integrity, and good sportsmanship when I play the sport I love. I *understand* only one team can win, but as long as I play with a *purpose* and will and give it all I have, then I have done my job."

The coach smiled. "Level up, huh? I'm going to use that with my players. Thanks. Great way to be a winner."

After the game, Mike Jr. raced Tim to the car for the front seat.

Knowing how happy Tim would be to sit in the front seat with the coach, Mike Jr. let him win.

The ride home was quiet. There was no music playing. Tim looked over his shoulder to see what Mike Jr. was doing.

He was surprised to see Mike was working on a science project that wasn't due for a week.

"Mike Jr., how can you do homework after a loss like that?"

"You must level up when you don't feel like it and even when no one is watching to get the results you want," Mike Jr. said. "Tim, no one knows that I have shot that shot over 10,000 times before. I was focused and wanted the ball in my hands. However, I missed the shot and still had to 'level up' in the moment. I *understood* that my team needed me to make the best play to give us a better chance to win. My purpose was to show that my hard work and skillset paid off."

After a time, Tim said, "But you missed the shot.

"I gave it all I had," Mike Jr. said. "And left it on the court. Now, I have to take that same energy and apply it to my life. So, if I miss the shot, which is to score a 100 on the test, I will hit the next mark, which is to get a 96." Mike Jr. stressed, "But Tim, the goal is always to level up."

They arrived at Tim's house. Tim thanked the coach for taking him to the game and waved goodbye to them both.

He walked into his house, excited to tell his parents what he'd learned from Coach Mike and Mike Jr.

There was a new Tim, and it was time for him to level up!

Details were purposefully left out about these characters to stress that life is full of uncertainties, and we can't be discouraged. As you read this book, my hope is that you will learn to think critically and take the time to analyze yourself.

Chapter 1: Focus Points

Why do you play basketball?

Who got you started in the sport?

Who do you look up to that plays the sport?

How many hours a day do you practice?

What is your favorite subject in school? Why?

What do you plan to learn from the sport?

Who is your favorite basketball player?

What does *Level Up* mean?

What can help you become the best person you can be?

What did you learn from John, Tim, and Mike Jr.?

Dreams DO come true if you work hard enough!

"One and Done" for Archie Goodwin.

Chapter 2

Determine Your Why

For the Love of the Game

Half of those who play sports start because it's fun and gives them some enjoyable time away from home and school. The other half may begin after their parents—who envision their children being like or better than they were—put a ball in their hands and ask them to score on a basketball hook attached to the back of a door in their home.

After making their first basket, children can see how it fills their parents with joy and passion and creates a desire to make another and another to continue making their parents proud.

Later, when the children are old enough to play outside, the desire continues, and their skills grow as they learn to dribble and attempt to master the fundamentals of basketball.

The average ballplayer learns from watching older siblings or friends battle in the backyard playing games like 21, 3 on 3, or King of the Court. Every chance the young ballplayer gets to shoot a shot, when there's a break in the action, he or she takes advantage of the opportunity, shooting until one of the older siblings runs the younger sibling off the court.

When NBA or college basketball is on the television, most ballplayers or lovers of the sport are glued to the play-by-play on TV. Many young players imagine themselves being in that starting role.

These are generally the precursors to a player getting the first chance to hit the hardwood. The pee-wee or little-league games are played at a local gym that focuses on helping the community.

Give it your all and don't look back, but always remember why you are in the present.

Chapter 2: Focus Points

What was the reason you started playing the sport?

What family member did you look up to that played the sport?

Did you feel that you were good at the sport and why?

Do you remember your first organized game?

Do you feel you were a good teammate?

When did you feel on top of your game?

How did you feel after your first loss?

Do you feel you were pushed too hard at a young age?

When was your best game?

Did you enjoy middle-school sports? If so, why? What made it enjoyable?

Did you play or plan on playing high-school sports?

What do you think the difference is between little league and middle school?

What's the difference between AAU and high-school sports?

What have you learned from your past coaches?

What's the highest level at which you would like to play?

Do you know how much work it would take for you to get to that level?

Heading to the Final 4, no looking back.

Chapter 3

The Coaches' Zone

Many players get to the point where they are just unsure of what the coach wants from them or feel like the coach's style is overwhelming as they press for success.

This is the point where every player should re-evaluate why he or she is playing the sport and what he or she is trying to get out of playing.

Develop a role and make sure the coach and team can't go without your presence. Sometimes your role might be to score every time you touch the ball. Maybe you're meant to have a unique role of rebounding only. You could be asked just to show leadership by coming off the bench, playing a pivotal role in getting a defensive stop, or guarding the quickest player on the court.

You are now about to walk into *The Coaches' Zone*, a place to understand what is expected from players in different roles.

Coach Ramona McGee

School/Organization: Pulaski Heights Middle School

Coaching Experience: 24 Years

Coach Clark: If a player walks in the gym for tryouts and never played before, how does he or she make the team?

Coach McGee: Well, it's totally up to the coach to make that decision, and I've definitely had that happen in my years of coaching. I will look at the effort they put out and see if they try to do all the workouts or if they need an outlet in their lives to keep them out of trouble by doing something organized and with structure. They might need to feel wanted and to be a part of an organization, something positive. I will give them an opportunity, and who knows, they might turn out to be outstanding ballplayers.

Coach Clark: How can a player win the coach over in tryouts?

Coach McGee: A player can win me over with hard work, leadership, and dedication on and off the court. A player's mindset should be to work hard every time he or she steps foot on the court. Players should leave everything else aside and put in 110% on and off the court. They should want to improve and get better every day.

Hard work makes winners.

Coach Clark: What are your expectations for returning players?

Coach McGee: They need to be role models for the younger players, have leadership skills, and be positive at all times with no bad vibes because younger players will be watching every move they make and how they act as upperclassmen.

Coach Clark: What are the key roles for starters?

Coach McGee: Accountability, know your role on the court, do what you do best, be a leader, and get the flow of the game started off right.

Coach Clark: What are the academic requirements for the team?

Coach McGee: Athletes must keep their grades up and be eligible to participate. I stress to my players that if they're not taking care of business in the classroom, I definitely don't need them in the gym with me. A player should have a 2.5 GPA or better.

Coach Clark: What do you expect each player to bring to the table?

Coach McGee: Each player should bring a good attitude, a willingness to learn and get better, and knowledge of the game.

Coach Clark: What role do parents play in sports?

Coach McGee: The role of parents is to be parents and to support their kids, the team, and the coaches from the stands. They are not to try coaching or telling the coach what to do and how to do it. That's *zero tolerance* for me, and that will always be stressed in my parent meetings. Some parents will try you, but you have to let them know real quick. That's not acceptable, nor will it be tolerated on this team.

Coach Clark: What are the biggest differences between the level of players?

Coach McGee: The biggest difference to me would be player development on the levels of middle to high school and college. Also, skillset and game management.

Coach Marcus D. Davis

School/Organization: Cloverdale Jr. High/Middle School

Coaching Experience: 36 years Little Rock School District

Coach Clark: How do you know if a player is prepared to play at his grade level?

Coach Davis: By their understanding of the fundamentals of the game and knowing their strengths and weaknesses.

Coach Clark: What are the strengths/weaknesses at your level for most players?

Coach Davis:

Strengths: Commitment and loyalty

Weaknesses: Not focusing on the details of the game, the fundamentals.

Coach Clark: If a player you've never seen before walks into the gym for tryouts, how does he make the team?

Coach Davis: By being coachable, listening to his coaches, working hard, competing to the best of his ability in every drill, and controlling what he can control: attitude, concentration, and effort.

Coach Clark: How can a player win the coach over in tryouts?

Coach Davis: He must have a competitive drive and be able to focus on developing fundamental skills. Don't be a showoff, and find a creative way to stand out.

Coach Clark: What should a player's mindset be when he has made the team and is preparing for practice?

Coach Davis: Be a leader on and off the floor, give maximum effort daily, and enjoy the experience.

Coach Clark: What are three keys for every player to look for at tryouts?

Coach Davis: Be prepared, be in shape, and be coachable.

Coach Clark: What is the expectation for returning players?

Coach Davis: Good leadership and establishing a positive relationship with all team members.

Coach Clark: What are the key roles for starters?

Coach Davis: Be accountable, step up and be a leader daily, and make all decisions in the team's best interest on and off the floor.

Coach Clark: What are the academic requirements for the team?

Coach Davis: There are no set requirements at this level, but I encourage our students/athletes to maintain a 3.0 GPA.

Coach Clark: What do you expect each player to bring to the table?

Coach Davis: Emphasize the team, not individuals. Be willing to put exceptional amounts of time into their craft daily.

Coach Clark: What is the expectation for a sub or the 6th man coming off the bench?

Coach Davis: Be competitive and do your job on both ends of the floor.

Coach Clark: How important is development at the level you're coaching, and what development do you see the most of at your level physically, mentally, and emotionally?

Coach Davis: Ability to shoot, dribble, pass, defend, and rebound are all skills required to be an effective ballplayer at this level.

Coach Clark: What are the parents' roles, and do the parents cross roles at times?

Coach Davis: The role of parents should be to help our students/athletes reach their personal and educational goals.

Coach Clark: What is the biggest difference between middle school, high school, and college?

Coach Davis: The higher-level schools are more intense in their training. The talent level is much more competitive. Your parents are there to help guide you in the lower levels, but in college, you quickly learn how to manage your responsibilities.

Coach Ray Barefield

School/Organization: Rancho Christian (*Boys Varsity Basketball*)

Coaching Experience: 20 + years of AAU, HS, "Mobley Brothers," Evan and Isaiah Mobley—USC top 10 NBA prospect, Dominic Harris—Gonzaga, Sedrick Barefield—Utah/ NBA G League, Jaden Byers—UOP HC Damon Stoudemire

Coach Clark: How do you know if a player is prepared to play at his grade level?

Coach Barefield: I evaluate based on a kid's potential, the current level of skill, athleticism, size, IQ, and mental makeup. I always go by the "Hourglass Approach," slow and over time vs. quick. Is he on track for his true potential?

Coach Clark: What are the strengths/weaknesses at your level for most players?

Coach Barefield: I coach a wide variety of kids, ranging from guys who will have a good HS experience playing the game to kids that will play NAIA, D3, D2, D1, and NBA. Most kids, early on, lack fundamentals and skills. Also, many are unaware of defensive principles and proper techniques with feet and hands.

Coach Clark: If a player you've never seen before walks into the gym for tryouts, how does he make the team?

Coach Barefield: I think first impressions are key. Work ethic, professionalism, and etiquette make a big impression. "Yes, Sir. No, Sir. Thank you, Coach." Be a fan of your teammates, have energy, and show enthusiasm.

Coach Clark: How can a player win the coach over in tryouts?

Coach Barefield: Be vocal; don't be afraid to fail or to take extra reps to get better. Encourage teammates, hustle, work hard, listen, and adjust after being corrected.

Coach Clark: What should a player's mindset be when he has made the team and is preparing for practice?

Coach Barefield: I think the most important thing is a commitment to the team and himself to get better daily.

Coach Clark: What are the three keys every player should look for at tryouts?

Coach Barefield: Culture, work ethic, and organization.

Coach Clark: What is the expectation for returning players?

Coach Barefield: Returners are expected to lead and set the standard and example for all the newcomers to model.

Coach Clark: What are the key roles for starters?

Coach Barefield: Leadership, police the team, set goals, and hold others accountable to the standards needed to match a given goal.

Coach Antonio Buchanan

School/Organization: Buchanan Mentality/Woods Elite

Coaching Experience: 11 Years

Coach Clark: How do you evaluate if a player can play at your level?

Coach Buchanan: I am realistic with them about their current skill sets, and I express to them to keep working on their game.

Coach Clark: What are the strengths/weaknesses at your level for most players?

Coach Buchanan: Mindset, pro skill set, and size are strengths on the circuit. The weakness is that most players have good skill sets but no IQ.

Coach Clark: If a player you've never seen before walks into the gym for tryouts, how does he make the team?

Coach Buchanan: First off, I'm fair to everyone who walks into my gym. If you are coming in underrated, you have to come in and show that you belong in the gym. Work harder than other people, play the game the right way, and show your talent.

Coach Clark: How can a player win the coach over in tryouts?

Coach Buchanan: By coming in and working harder than other people and catching on quickly to what the coach is teaching.

Coach Clark: What should a player's mindset be after he has made the team and is preparing for practice?

Coach Buchanan: Killer mindset, Buchanan Mentality (laughs), meaning I'm going at everyone, every day. Be a good teammate, compete in every way, and be coachable.

Coach Clark: What are three keys every player should look for at tryouts?

Coach Buchanan: Tempo, working hard, and being uncomfortable to become comfortable.

Coach Clark: What is the expectation for returning players?

Coach Buchanan: Lead by example. Show players why they're still on the team.

Coach Clark: What are the key roles for starters?

Coach Buchanan: Set the tone and set themselves apart from everyone else.

Coach Clark: What are the academic requirements for the team?

Coach Buchanan: They are the same as the NCAA

requirements.

Coach Clark: What do you expect each player to bring to the table?

Coach Buchanan: Being coachable and willing to work hard.

Coach Clark: What GPA does a player have to have each semester?

Coach Buchanan: We adhere to the GPA in the NCAA requirements.

Coach Clark: What is the expectation for a sub or the 6th man coming off the bench?

Coach Buchanan: Either pick the starters up or pick up where they left off if they were already playing well.

Coach Clark: How important is development at the level you're coaching, and what development do you see the most of at your level physically, mentally, and emotionally?

Coach Buchanan: Development is very important. I coach in the toughest league. So, you have to get better every year, or you will get rolled over physically and emotionally.

Coach Clark: What are the roles for the parents, and do the parents cross roles at times?

Coach Buchanan: Just be the parent. Let me be the coach and trainer. If not, they can coach and train their kids.

Coach Clark: What is the biggest difference between middle school, high school, and college basketball?

Coach Buchanan: Maturity.

Coach Daryl Fimple

School/University: North Little Rock School District

Coaching Experience: Overall Record: (22 Years): 495-131, Record at NLR: 343-70 (14 Years)

Coach Clark: How do you evaluate if a player can play at your level?

Coach Fimple: We have a template of required skills for athletes from grades 7th through 12th. Each athlete is evaluated every season to see if his skill level is improving. The template deals with the basic skills of shooting, dribbling, and passing. At the end of each athlete's season, the athlete is given a personal evaluation. This enables the athlete to see his strengths and weaknesses from year to year. With improvement, athletes advance to the next year, where required skills are added that are more complex. We call these player prescriptions. It's a prescription or a blueprint of improving from one year to the next. The older the athletes get, the more precise we get with adding to their skill sets.

Coach Clark: If a player you have never seen before walks into the gym for tryouts, how does he make the team?

Coach Fimple: Each level of our tryout system is devoted to finding what skills any athlete possesses that fit our template. All of our tryouts are filmed and looked at to determine how that athlete could help the team. If a player walks in whom we do not know of, we will determine his skill set with what our template says a player should know skill-wise. Since each template is considered to be grade-level appropriate, it is translated to each athlete on that grade level. Tryouts are also broken down into skill levels by the entire coaching staff.

Coach Clark: How can a player win the coach over in tryouts?

Coach Fimple: Being skilled is always great, but if an athlete can show leadership qualities, a strong work ethic, and the ability to be coached, those characteristics always play a part in a tryout setting.

Coach Clark: What should a player's mindset be when he has made the team and is preparing for practice?

Coach Fimple: Practice will be intense, so an athlete has to be ready to give 100 percent mentally and physically. Practice is never longer than one hour and thirty minutes. Usually, it occurs at the end of the school day, so school distractions are put to the side. We try to explain to kids that drills are where you get to create your skills. Each drill is explained to the fullest, so athletes know exactly what we are looking for. The other thing is making sure athletes are not comfortable where they are or are coasting. Athletes have to be pushed, so the tempo of practice is at a high rate of efficiency and planning.

Coach Clark: What are three keys every player should look for at tryouts?

Coach Fimple: We are looking for athletes who give great effort, engage with teammates, and are willing to work.

1. Do players show the ability to compete? EX. 1/1, 2/2, 3/3, 4/4, 5/5. Do their teams win?

2. Do players use their skills to benefit their teams? Do they make their teams better?

3. Does the player control the controllable?

Coach Clark: What is the expectation for returning players?

Coach Fimple: Returning players are made to go through the entire tryout process. Looking at kids moving up from JV to Varsity level is a huge jump.

Coach Clark: What are the key roles for starters?

Coach Fimple: The big thing about starters is keeping practice competitive. We arrange our practices daily, where we mix and match lineups all the time. It keeps kids locked in on performance daily. We even have weight room partners change weekly. The big key is that starters sometimes aren't just your best players. They might be your best rebounders, defenders, screeners, or leaders.

Coach Clark: What are the academic requirements for the team?

Coach Fimple: We have been blessed with amazing student-athletes. Last year's GPA was 3.6. We usually shoot for a 3.0 or above.

Coach Clark: What do you expect each player to bring to the table daily?

Coach Fimple: Discipline, dedication, ability to focus, work ethic, and a hard hat mentality.

Coach Clark: What are the expectations for the sub or the 6th man coming off the bench?

Coach Fimple: You will have an amazing team if your bench can provide you with energy and the ability to change the game in some aspect. It could be on offense, defense, rebounding, or being able to pick your teammates up.

Coach Clark: How important is development at the level you coach, and what development do you see the most of at your level physically, mentally, and emotionally?

Coach Fimple: Mental and emotional maturity usually happens by graduation.

Coach Clark: What are the roles of the parents, and do the parents cross roles at times?

Coach Fimple: Parents' roles should be that of support for not only their athletes but the support of the team and coaches. Parents have crossed the line in trying to make it easy for their athletes. It's a process that takes growth and, more importantly, patience. From year to year, a kid's role can change through their performance in practice. Coaches have favorites; they love the kids who are loyal hard-workers.

Coaches play kids to give their teams the best chance to win.

Coach Clark: What is the biggest difference between middle school, high school, and college?

Coach Fimple: Always, the work gets harder level to level. Also, competition in high-school girls' basketball is overwhelming. Over 6 million girls play high-school basketball inside the U.S. alone. Only 1% of those athletes will play college basketball on scholarship.

Coach Marland Smith

School/Organization: Dermott High School/Team South

Coaching Experience: High-School Basketball Coach for four years. Record: 123-57

Coach Clark: How do you evaluate if a player can play at your level?

Coach Smith: Work ethic is the key! So many kids have the talent to play at that level but don't have the work ethic.

Coach Clark: What are the strengths/weaknesses at your level for most players?

Coach Smith: IQ. I don't think players realize how much the game changes when you strengthen your IQ.

Coach Clark: If a player you've never seen before walks into the gym for tryouts, how does he make the team?

Coach Smith: First thing is to be yourself. Stick to your strengths! As a coach/evaluator, I can tell if a kid can play or not after two or three trips up the court and by whether he makes a shot or not!

Coach Clark: How can a player win the coach over in tryouts?

Coach Smith: As a coach, I look for players who can help me win games! There are so many things we need as coaches to help make our team successful. What players have to realize is that being able to score doesn't always help win games. I've had kids who couldn't shoot, dribble, or pass well, but they knew how to get teammates open. They were always in the right spots on defense, they blocked out, and took charges. Those are the things I look for.

Coach Clark: What should a player's mindset be when he has made the team and is preparing for practice?

Coach Smith: Practice is key! If we can't get things right at practice, how can/will we get things done in a game? It doesn't work that way! As a coach, I put all of my work into practice. I'm more dedicated to practices than I am to games!

Coach Clark: What are three keys every player should look for at tryouts?

Coach Smith: Leadership, hard work, and winning.

Coach Clark: What is the expectation for returning players?

Coach Smith: I expect my returners to be leaders. I expect them to lead by example. You've been in the system, so you should know what to expect!

Coach Clark: What are the key roles for starters?

Coach Smith: It varies! I feel my starters are predicated on what's best for the team! There have been times when my best scorers have come off the bench. If that's needed for us to be the best team possible, then that's what I will do.

Coach Clark: What are the academic requirements for the team?

Coach Smith: Academics are important! If we are talking in terms of high schoolers getting to college, then academics should be a top priority. You can't get to the next level without the right grades.

Coach Clark: What do you expect each player to bring to the table?

Coach Smith: Each player is required to bring something different to the table. To me, it depends on that player's strengths. I've seemed to have more success when I create a game plan designed around my players' strengths.

Coach Clark: What GPA does a player have to have each semester?

Coach Smith: In high school, you have to maintain a C average, which is a 2.0.

Coach Clark: What is the expectation for the sub or the 6th man coming off the bench?

Coach Smith: How important is development at the level you're coaching, and what development do you see the most of at your level physically, mentally, and emotionally?

Coach Clark: What are the roles of the parents, and do the parents cross roles at times?

Coach Smith: This is a tough topic because parents can be overwhelming. But it's important to have that kind of relationship with your parents. You want them to trust you. And if they are going to trust you with their kids, then they have to trust everything you do!

Coach Clark: What is the biggest difference between middle school, high school, and college?

Coach Smith: The difference from middle school to high school is that you have 12- to 13-year-olds playing with 17- to 18-years-olds. That's a big gap! Middle school kids can't compare body-wise.

High school to college is a bit different. When you get to college, everyone is good! Everyone was the best in high school. I tell my kids all the time. There's one thing that can separate you when the talent level is even, and that's IQ! The team/player who plays smarter will be more successful!

Coach Marlon Staton Jr. (Coach Pop)

School/Organization: GetMeRecruited (President of Basketball Operations/Director of Scouting)

Coaching Experience: High School & AAU

Coach Clark: How do you evaluate if a player can play at your level?

Coach Pop: Footwork, attitude, motor, & skillset.

- Always watch from the feet up. Elite players have elite footwork.
- Are they coachable? Do they listen?
- Do they play to win, and do they play hard?
- How good is their overall skillset?

Coach Clark: What are the strengths/weaknesses at your level for most players?

Coach Pop:

- Work ethic.
- Kids don't have blueprints on how to get better.

Coach Clark: If a player you have never seen before walks into the gym for tryouts, how does he make the team?

Coach Pop:

- Communicate.
- Play hard.
- Lock up on defense.

Coach Clark: How can a player win the coach over in tryouts?

Coach Pop:

- Communicate.
- Play hard.
- Lock up on defense.
- Make the simple plays.

Coach Clark: What should a player's mindset be when he has made the team and is preparing for practice?

Coach Pop:

- Improve every day.
- Be the hardest worker in practice.

Coach Clark: What are three keys every player should look for at tryouts?

Coach Pop:

- Communicate—it takes the least talent and goes the farthest.
- Be a good teammate—nobody wants to play with an butt hole.
- Always play hard—energy is contagious, and coaches love players who play hard.

Coach Clark: What is the expectation for returning players?

Coach Pop: You HAVE to set an example.

Coach Clark: What are the key roles for starters?

Coach Pop:

- Set an example.
- Know your role—rebounders rebound, point guards run the team, and shooters shoot.
- Hold each other accountable.

Coach Clark: What are the academic requirements for the team?

Coach Pop:

- 3.5 + no mandatory tutoring.
- 3.5 - mandatory daily tutoring.

Coach Clark: What do you expect each player to bring to the table?

Coach Pop:

- Willingness to work.
- Great attitude.
- Want to learn and get better.
- MUST PLAY HARD.

Coach Clark: What GPA does a player have to have each semester?

Coach Pop:

- 2.8.

Coach Clark: What is the expectation for the sub or the 6th man coming off the bench?

Coach Pop:
- Know the tendencies of whom you're guarding—while on the bench, study them to see what you can pick up to help you defend them.
- No drop-off—come in ready to contribute.
- Always stay positive.

Coach Clark: How important is development at the level you're coaching, and what development do you see the most at your level physically, mentally, and emotionally?

Coach Pop:
- Development is the key to every program. The good kids want to get better. Development has to be a part of your culture.
- All three types of development, physical, mental, and emotional, are just as important.

Coach Clark: What are the roles of the parents, and do the parents cross roles at times?

Coach Pop:
- Make sure you're supporting your child, but don't overdo it.
- Be honest with your child—not everybody is going to play High Major basketball.
- Don't take the fun out of it for your kid.
- DO NOT be the parent who bugs the coach or scouts—let your kid's game do the talking.

Coach Clark: What is the biggest difference between middle school, high school, and college?

Coach Pop:

- Skill level and dedication.
- Players' bodies start to catch up with them.
- Skillsets become more important than athleticism.
- Speed of the game.
- Everyone is good in middle school.

Coach Brandon Taylor

School/Organization: Grayson College

Coaching Experience: 10th year/178-96

Coach Clark: How do you evaluate if a player can play at your level?

Coach Taylor: My evaluation considerations look at athletes who can score at all three levels. The main focus is on the defensive side. The athlete must have a great stance on being down and ready with eyes locked in on feet and ball while communicating with the team on all accounts.

Coach Clark: What are the strengths/weaknesses at your level for most players?

Coach Taylor: For athletes at this level, the strengths are that they have an opportunity to get ahead and learn a lot of the lingo for high-level basketball before they reach the NCAA level.

Weaknesses are usually mental, so we work to increase their mental strength.

Coach Clark: If a player you have never seen before walks into the gym for tryouts, how does he make the team?

Coach Taylor: If a player walks into the gym for tryouts whom I've never seen before, the player must possess an EXCELLENT work ethic, must show that he is hungry, must want to be a student of the game, and must have a great basketball IQ.

Coach Clark: What should a player's mindset be when he has made the team and is preparing for practice?

Coach Taylor: I believe that the player must come in ready to work and become great. With a great mindset for preparation comes a great mindset for winning and being successful.

Coach Clark: What are three keys every player should look for at tryouts?

Coach Taylor: Three keys for every player should be as follows:

1) Come in ready to work and do what it takes to get the job done.

2) Have a team mentality, along with a very small portion of personal goals.

3) Be able to communicate and prove that they can handle this game.

Coach Clark: What is the expectation for returning players?

Coach Taylor: If you want to play, you must show and prove that you can do all the little things that will make this team successful. For example, showing leadership while being a returner, communication is key, aggressive defensively, and attacking offensively.

Coach Clark: What are the key roles for starters?

Coach Taylor: (no response)

Coach Clark: What are the academic requirements for the team?

Coach Taylor: We have high standards academically because the NCAA has changed a lot of the requirements for student-athletes. Also, because without the grades or a degree, you cannot play. We look at having a team GPA of 2.8-3.6. The reason is that we know some kids struggle in classroom settings and need a little extra help as far as tutoring. The 3.6 is because, at the juco level, the players are taking a majority of core classes: math, science, history, and English. Some come from schools that offered a great academic structure.

Coach Clark: What do you expect each player to bring to the table?

Coach Taylor: I expect each player to bring it every day and to look for success, whether it is in practice or the classroom. I expect them to be great people in the community and on campus. Everybody's watching everybody else at all times.

Coach Clark: What GPA does a player have to have each semester?

Coach Taylor: A player must maintain a minimum of 2.7.

Coach Clark: What is the expectation for the sub or the 6th man coming off the bench?

Coach Taylor: Expectations for subs in our rotations are that they come off the bench ready to increase the intensity and power of play. Positive energy is everything in this game.

Coach Clark: How important is development at the level you're coaching, and what development do you see the most of at your level physically, mentally, and emotionally?

Coach Taylor: Player development is everything now because some kids need more breakdowns before they can see action. Personally, I would love to have a kid who comes in and has some skill because, at the juco level, we don't have much time to prepare before it's go time. As far as which development I see most from all three levels, I'd say physical and mental because we push them beyond their levels of thinking. They are also pushed emotionally because sometimes the kid or kids have emotional breakdowns because they don't think they're doing enough or something has happened inside the family.

Coach Clark: What are the roles of the parents, and do the parents cross roles at times?

Coach Taylor: I simply believe that there is nothing wrong with parents supporting their kids. But for a kid to grow as an athlete and person, the parents must simply let their kid endure some things. For example, a coach will yell at the kids and put the kids through the fire because this world outside of basketball can be a grueling world sometimes.

Coach Clark: What is the biggest difference between middle school, high school, and college?

Coach Taylor: The biggest difference between the three levels is that even though the work seems the same, the expectations and intensity go up quite a bit most of the time. Things change as far as vocabulary and coaches.

Coach Ronnie Williford

Former Collegiate Basketball Coach

Coaching Experience: 12 Years Collegiate Coaching Experience

Coach Clark: How do you evaluate if a player can play at your level?

Coach Williford: At the collegiate level, I evaluate a player's competitive spirit. Competitive spirit is transferred into one's ability to be aggressive at all times, offensively or defensively. The overly aggressive players are the players who maximize their gifts and talents. Aggression can be taught—the who, what, when, where, and how to.

Coach Clark: What are the strengths/weaknesses at your level for most players?

Coach Williford:

The Strengths: Players love to play games when the lights come on and the fans are watching.

The Weaknesses: The mental approach for preparing to compete at everything, every day… when I speak of mental approach, I speak of the WILL to learn how to apply skills to games/live situations effectively. The how to and when to do something are just as important as knowing what skill you are learning.

Coach Clark: If a player you have never seen before walks into the gym for tryouts, how does he make the team?

Coach Williford: EFFORT... compete... talent is not distributed equally. A player's effort of always encouraging possible teammates to work towards being 1st at everything during this particular tryout will grab the coach's attention in a good way.

Coach Clark: How can a player win the coach over in tryouts?

Coach Williford: EFFORT... compete... make an attempt to be 1st at everything during this timeframe. Always be encouraging.

Coach Clark: What should a player's mindset be when he has made the team and is preparing for practice?

Coach Williford: Be the best player in the gym that day. During every drill, work extremely hard to learn and apply it to games/live situations.

Coach Clark: What are three keys every player should look for at tryouts?

Coach Williford:

Key 1: Other Than You: Who Is the Best Player?

Key 2: Other Than You: Always Match Up with the Best Player

in Drills.

Key 3: Other Than You: Always Play on the Opposite Team of the Best Player.

Doing these things allows you to be in the coach's eyesight. In turn, you will have the ability to put your competitive spirit on full display.

Coach Clark: What is the expectation for returning players?

Coach Williford: The only expectation for returning players during tryouts is for them to be a good example of what the culture is in that particular program.

Coach Clark: What are the key roles for starters?

Coach Williford: The key roles for starters are always to get things going in a good position. Starters are the tone-setters. They set the tone day in and day out in everything that is done. Starters should make sure that they are setting the competitive tone.

Coach Clark: What are the academic requirements for the team?

Coach Williford: Academic requirements may vary per program. We would want our players to maintain an above 3.0-grade point average.

Coach Clark: What do you expect each player to bring to the table?

Coach Williford: This expectation will always begin with a competitive spirit. It will always end with a competitive spirit.

Coach Clark: What GPA does a player have to have each semester?

Coach Williford: Each semester, a player must maintain a 2.8 GPA.

Coach Clark: What is the expectation for a sub or the 6th man coming off the bench?

Coach Williford: Competitive spirit and awareness of what to do on the offensive and defensive end for that particular segment.

Coach Clark: How important is development at the level you're coaching, and what development do you see the most of at your level physically, mentally, and emotionally?

Coach Williford: The development phase is the lifeline of programs. It's highly important. There are not many God-gifted and naturally talented, *LeBron James*-like individuals. Physical development has been the mainstream of most programs. Moving forward, you will see the mental and emotional development thoroughly implemented. Being a top-tier competitor, you exhaust all aspects of these developments, physical, mental, and emotional.

Coach Clark: What are the roles of the parents, and do the parents cross roles at times?

Coach Williford: The parents' role is to support the competitor in being his best and competing at his very best.

Their role is to allow their children's effort and abilities to represent their results. Parents do cross this line because we have yet to understand how to go about supporting the competitor in certain situations. They want what is best for their children, and sometimes what's best for their children is to support them by telling them to ask for guidance from their coach and apply what they tell you with maximum effort.

Coach Clark: What is the biggest difference between middle school, high school, and college?

Coach Williford: The mental approach is important when competing because everyone is talented and skilled. The very best become the very best because they learn to love competition. Competing means learning the who, what, when, where, how, and why to every situation then applying that to live situations with maximum effort.

Coach Johnnie Harris

School/Organization: Head Coach at Auburn

Coaching Experience: 20th Year Associate/Assistant Head Coach

Coach Clark: How do you evaluate if a player can play at your level?

Coach Harris: We look for players who can fit into our system, players who are tough, hard-nosed, and aggressive, who can get downhill. They can create for themselves and their teammates. We look for players who run the floor with a tough mindset, as well as players who can score at will. We want the total package, a player with great character, a team player, and lastly, a player who is coachable to fit the system.

Coach Clark: What are the strengths/weaknesses for most players at your level?

Coach Harris: Starting with a point guard, they need to be strong communicators, to be able to handle the ball, to be strong leaders, and to be able to hold the team accountable when things are going wrong but also be able to give them praise when things are going great on and off the court. It is vital that the point guard has a great relationship with the coaching staff to understand and to be able to implement the coach's expectations. It is a strong bonus for a point guard. These two guards need to be able to shoot the ball and handle the ball. We like to run our two guards off-ball screens and to help the point guard bring the ball up when needed. The small forward slashes to the basket and look for post opportunities. We like for them to create opportunities for themselves and others and be more of a utility type of player.

A power forward needs to be a versatile player who can play like a point guard/forward, handle the ball, make shots, and drive strong to the basket. A power forward needs to rebound and deny the high post. Power forwards are some of the strongest players we have on the defensive end. Centers are tough. They need to grab rebounds, box out, dive hard to the basket, have good timing, have poise in the air, and have a good second jump.

As far as weaknesses go, most point guards don't shoot well or set the team up in offensive sets. Two guards don't come into the program handling the ball with precise control, and they come off the screen late, so they don't get the proper shot off. Small forwards come in just athletic but with few skills like ball handling, playmaking, and court appearance. Power forwards lack ball handling and skills shooting from 15 feet. They don't post up strong. Centers don't run the floor hard or cut to the basket. They don't post deep, and they lack the ability to pass or find the open man or cutter.

Coach Clark: How can you win a coach over?

Coach Harris: Do you play hard? Are you a team player? Will you take charge? Are you coachable? Also, how a player responds when he is taken out of the game can make an impression. Do they still clap for teammates, or is it all about them? How they communicate with the coaches and teammates, as well as how their body language is during and after the game, matters.

First, you win the coach's attention with how you are playing, and you keep the coach's attention by how you are acting. This is a key factor when the staff is considering bringing you into our family.

Coach Clark: What should a player's mindset be when he has made the team and is preparing for practice?

Coach Harris: Practice with the mindset of trying to stand out. It's just another tryout, so keep your mindset and skills sharp. Walk into every practice with a will to win that day. A player's mindset should be focused on getting better and making the team better.

Coach Clark: What are three keys everyone should look for in tryouts?

Coach Harris: Players must be competitive. Finding the best player and competing at a high level is crucial. Next is being coachable. Know what they want from each player and be able to execute on both ends of the court. Finally, being a team player and knowing your role is necessary.

Coach Clark: What is the key role for starters?

Coach Harris: Starters need to come in with a championship mentality, have a will to come in early, and be the last ones to leave the gym. Starters must have respect for the bench players, and they need to learn how to be an extension of the coach.

Coach Clark: What are the academic requirements for the team?

Coach Harris: Academically, we require a 2.75 minimum, but our expectation is a 3.0. We push our student-athletes to accomplish this by having academic meetings, talking to our academic counselor, and reaching this goal by attending study hall or extra tutoring.

Coach Clark: What do you expect each player to bring to the table?

Coach Harris: Be ready to compete daily and have a championship mindset daily. Act like professionals, be on time, get the work done, and be masters of their craft.

Coach Clark: What is the expectation of a sub or the 6th man off the bench?

Coach Harris: Come and work hard. Ensure there's no drop-off in performance, and if the team is down, bring some energy to the game.

Coach Clark: How important is development at the level you're coaching mentally, physically, and emotionally?

Coach Harris: Development is important for the team to grow and for everyone to be able to impact the game. At this level, we have the right resources that focus on each of these areas to help our student-athletes to be well-rounded in life and basketball.

Coach Eric Musselman

School/Organization: University of Arkansas

Coaching Experience:

- Head Coach of Golden State Warriors and Sacramento Kings
- Head Coach of University of Nevada
- Current Head Coach of the University of Arkansas

Coach Clark: How do you evaluate if a player can play at your level?

Coach Musselman: We look for length 1-5, skill set, shooting, ball handling, and versatility. Can a guy guard multiple positions?

Coach Clark: What are the strengths/weaknesses at your level for most players?

Coach Musselman:

Strengths: Shooting, versatility, playing hard, athleticism, and quickness.

Weaknesses: Skilled big men and being able to guard multiple positions.

Coach Clark: If a player you have never seen before walks into the gym for tryouts, how does he make the team?

Coach Musselman: Playing hard, shooting the ball, and being able to do a multitude of things. Versatility is something that stands out.

Coach Clark: How can a player win the coach over in tryouts?

Coach Musselman: How hard do they play, and are they coachable? Can they apply what is put into a drill or a teaching point?

Coach Clark: What should a player's mindset be when he has made the team and is preparing for practice?

Coach Musselman: How do I get better today? How can I help the team get better today?

Coach Clark: What are three keys for every player to look for at tryouts?

Coach Musselman: Coachability, work ethic, and shooting ability.

Coach Clark: What is the expectation for returning players?

Coach Musselman: How well can they make the jump from Year 1 to Year 2? There shouldn't ever be any regression with returning players.

Coach Clark: What are the key roles for starters?

Coach Musselman: Starting the game with the lead, at the first media timeout, we never want to be in a hole. Set the tone of the game. Limit turnovers and make the simple plays to start the game.

Coach Clark: What are the academic requirements for the team?

Coach Musselman: Everyone must have at least a 2.0 GPA. We have different academic requirements for different players. Some guys are more academically capable than others. We want each individual to be pushed to his max academically.

Coach Clark: What is the expectation for the sub or the 6th man coming off the bench?

Coach Musselman: Change of pace, bring something different to the game. We like to have someone who would be a "good starter," come off the bench to give us a little bit of an extra punch.

Coach Clark: How important is development at the level you're coaching, and what development do you see the most of at your level physically, mentally, and emotionally?

Coach Musselman: Development is extremely important. We want guys who love to be in the gym. If you don't love the game of basketball or want to get better, you will have a tough time being successful.

Coach Clark: What are the roles of the parents, and do the parents cross roles at times?

Coach Musselman: The role of parents is vital. We want them to be engaged in all aspects of the student-athlete's life.

Coach Clark: What is the biggest difference between middle school, high school, and college basketball?

Coach Musselman: Skill level and athleticism, each time a player jumps up a level, there are more and more hurdles. When a player makes the jump from being the best player on his HS team, he's going to play with 10-11 other players on his college team that were also the best players on their high-school teams.

Coach Jermaine Johnson

School/Organization: Troy University

Coaching Experience:

- Student Assistant Coach at Memphis
- Head Coach Memphis Melrose High School
- Assistant Coach at Georgia Southern
- Associate Head Coach at the University of Tennessee Martin
- Current Assistant Coach at Troy University

Coach Clark: How do you evaluate if a player can play at your level?

Coach Johnson: We look for length 1-5: skill set, shooting, ball handling, passing, and IQ with versatility.

Coach Clark: What is the strength/weakness at your level for most players?

Coach Johnson:

Strengths: Shooting, toughness, playing hard, athleticism, and attacking the paint.

Weaknesses: Skilled big men, being able to guard multiple

positions, and willing passers.

Coach Clark: If a player you've never seen before walks into the gym for tryouts, how does he make the team?

Coach Johnson: Playing hard, shooting the ball, and being able to do a multitude of things; versatility is a gift, and that's what we look for.

Coach Clark: How can a player win the coach over in tryouts?

Coach Johnson: How hard do they play, and are they coachable? Can they make applicable those skills that were learned?

Coach Clark: What should a player's mindset be when he has made the team and is preparing for practice?

Coach Johnson: How do I get better today? How can I help the team get better today?

Coach Clark: What are three keys every player should look for at tryouts?

Coach Johnson: Coachability, intrinsic work ethic, and shot-making ability.

Coach Clark: What is the expectation for returning players?

Coach Johnson: How well can they make the jump from Year 1 to Year 3?

Coach Clark: What are the key roles for starters?

Coach Johnson: Starting the game out with the lead, at

the first media timeout, we never want to be in down. Be relentless with effort and toughness. Limit turnovers and make the right plays to start the game.

Coach Clark: What are the academic requirements for the team?

Coach Johnson: Everyone must have at least a 2.0 GPA. We have different academic requirements for different players. We want everyone to be challenged individually.

Coach Clark: What is the expectation for a sub or the 6th man coming off the bench?

Coach Johnson: Change of pace, bring something different to the game.

Chapter 3: Focus Points

What was the very first point you learned from the coaches?

How hard do you feel it is to coach?

Now, how hard is it for someone to coach you?

Are you willing to better your best daily?

Are you willing to focus more on the impact you bring to the team?

Photo Gallery

Coach Sammy Clark

Sammy Clark was able to help get Connors State College (Warner, Oklahoma) back on the map by helping the team keep a top 25 ranking all year and get back to the national tournament.

Sammy Clark with one of the greatest coaches in college basketball, Phillip Martelli, who helped lead Michigan back to the Elite 8.

Sammy Clark with Naismith Hall of Fame Coach Kim Mulkey who earned National Coach of the Year twice with 2 NCAA Women Championships.

Sammy Clark with Coach Mike Davis, who turned the UAB program around.

Sammy Clark with Joshua Pastner, who became the head coach behind Coach Cal for the University of Memphis and now has been led to turn around Georgia Tech.

Sammy Clark with Scott Drew of the Baylor Men's Basketball program, which has been recognized as one of the top programs in the nation!

Sammy Clark with Jerry Mullen at Mullens Junior College All-Star Camp.

Sammy Clark with Darrell Walker, current Head Coach for the University of Arkansas at Little Rock.

Sammy Clark with Scotty Mason hosting a National Basketball Camp.

Sammy Clark working out some of Arkansas' top players who are being looked at by colleges.

Sammy Clark working out with Andre Clark and NBA Super Star, Joe Johnson, helping give the young man a few pointers before his Dunbar summer league game.

Sammy Clark with A.J. Walton, Archie Goodwin, and CJ Nash.

Sammy Clark with **Nyeshia "Ny" Stevenson.**

Sammy Clark supporting some of Arkansas' best basketball players.

Sammy Clark with Shekinna Stricklen who was working hard to prepare for the University of Tennessee. She worked her way to becoming the Number 2 pick in the WNBA draft.

Don Williams and Sammy Clark with the number 13 overall NBA draft pick, Corliss Williamson—one of the best players to ever play at the University of Arkansas, developing some of the top players across the nation.

Chapter 4

Tryouts

Give It Your All. Don't Look Back.

The Tryout Stage

A player should be willing to work hard during the tryout. Show the coach his knowledge of the game.

Tryouts are when a player makes a statement for the new year. At this point, the coaching staff focuses on what adjustments need to be made to have a successful season.

The Coaching Staff

By the start of tryouts, the head coach focuses on what made the team successful or unsuccessful. The coach starts to develop a plan for improving the team and what will help with the team's growth.

Most coaches start building by asking these simple but important questions: who, what, when, where, how, and why (reason). Who is the competition, and how well do we match up as a team? Do we have a strong history of winning or losing a hard return? Note to the players: GO HARD!

Chapter 4: Focus Points

Are you willing to be persistent at working hard to get a spot on the team?

The day before tryouts, do some self-talk: "I will work hard. I will guard the best player on the team."

Are you willing to do the small stuff?

Are you willing to guard the best player on the court?

Are you willing to be in the top 3-line drills?

Identify how you can help the team.

What skillset do you bring to the table?

Chapter 5

Mental Toughness

Developing Resilience and Confidence

Mental toughness in sports is defined as the level of an individual's resilience, confidence, and thought processes. This toughness may predict one's success in sports, education, and professional environments. In sports, this concept is associated with coping abilities to handle pressure and uncertain situations, distractions, communication, etc.

Signs of Mental Toughness

The signs of players showing mental toughness are described below:

Influence/Control. They focus on areas where they have some level of influence or control (e.g., attitude, an athlete has a choice to engage in prosocial behaviors).

Thoughts. They regulate their thoughts and emotions so they can continue to perform consistently as opposed to reacting to their environments (e.g., a referee makes a bad call, and instead of just reacting, mentally tough athletes would regulate their frustrations to maintain optimal performances). This type of athlete can maneuver through unfavorable situations more productively.

Mindset. When approaching a new skill or task, athletes who show mental toughness approach those situations with a growth mindset. They display maximum effort, are open to receive feedback from coaches and/or peers, and persist in the face of setbacks (e.g., recovering from an injury) (Dweck, 2006).

Goals/Vision. Creating goals or a vision allows mentally tough athletes to stay focused, energized, and motivated. Creating goals per season, practice, and playing in games provide an opportunity for athletes to minimize distractions.

Confidence Level. Athletes should be able to adjust their confidence levels; some players experience high and low confidence over time. Mentally tough athletes recognize their levels and take the initiative to build their confidence by listening to Ted Talks or motivational speakers, pep talks, reading an inspirational quote, or playing their walkout theme song.

Signs of Mental Fatigue

Mental fatigue is when athletes find it hard or challenging to focus either during practice, games, or at home. The signs of mental fatigue are described below:

Staleness. Staleness in sports is defined as overtraining physically and mentally, and it wears on the body, which means the athlete isn't improving or getting better.

Motivation. The loss of motivation to play.

Quality. Quality of performances decreases.

Yielding to Pressure. This occurs when the athlete is experiencing consistent pressure (e.g., to win or maintain scholarship) or is subjected to unfulfilled/inappropriate expectations (e.g., over-emphasis on recruitment or ranks).

Communication. The athlete communicates that he or she is mentally and physically exhausted.

Ways Players Can Challenge Themselves

Players can challenge themselves by following the tips described below:

Awareness. Recognize their pressure points and incorporate them into their practices to help familiarize themselves with those situations or moments. This strategy best prepares the athlete for when those situations happen in the game. He or she will be ready (e.g., on the free-throw line with 5 seconds on the clock down by 1).

Practice. Practice how you play. Athletes who treat practice like games will allow their skills to have a smoother transition for an authentic performance.

Visualize. Using visualization or mental rehearsal can help athletes learn a new skill or better their performances. Athletes who practice visualization before and after performances stimulate the brain regions. Similarly, if they were physically performing, the athletes could learn from their mistakes or condition their minds for successful outcomes.

Comfort. Train yourself to be comfortable with being uncomfortable.

Recognizing Mental Overload

Mental overload occurs when an athlete attempts to process too much information at one time.

Often, athletes will notice physical before mental overload because it is easy to tune into bodily feedback as opposed to focusing on their thinking.

However, every athlete's signs and symptoms of mental overload can vary. It is best for the athlete to prevent mental overload by focusing on one thing at a time. It is also helpful for athletes to engage or participate in tasks that are the opposite of those from which they are recovering.

For example, to recover from reading or studying, for 4 to 6 hours, the athlete should participate in a task that is not cognitively demanding, such as a walk or a run.

Practicing Mental Development

Preparing for mental toughness is very individualized, especially at different experience levels. When referencing mental toughness, there is no one size fits all. Athletes have different levels of mental toughness. The best way to practice mental development is to become familiar with mental training. There are many great books that provide insight into training the mind or seeking personal training.

Chapter 5: Focus Points

Are you willing to wake up and run a mile 3 times a week?

Are you willing to make a key play in the games that will cause a win or a loss?

Are you able to be positive when things are not going your way?

Are you willing to study the sport you say you love to play?

Are you willing to challenge yourself daily?

Note: Athletes can locate the nearest mental performance consultant on the widely recognized psychology website, Association Applied Sport Psychology (AASP).

Re'Aunna Henderson, MS.

Notes of Wisdom:

Be real with yourself.

Allow your results to speak for themselves.

Love what you do.

Better your best.

Nyeshia Stevenson demonstrating that you are not limited to just one sport.

AJ Walton "going to work" in an Arkansas State Tournament.

Chapter 6

Developing Your Skills

Practice Makes Perfect!

It's essential to come to every practice with a mindset to compete at a high level. This means working hard, focusing on communication, understanding the coach's system, and going all-in every drill.

A player must understand that the coach wants the team to be at their best, so they will get pushed to the max by great coaches. Players must find what they are good at and play on it, every drill. You must still do the things you are not great at, but don't just focus on them. Do your best and level up. Have a strong work ethic and let no one beat you in a line drill or hustling to a loose ball.

Learn the offensive and defensive systems. Practice with a chip on your shoulder, and let your friends see your focus and leadership skills. Be committed to the process of greatness; your inner drive will open up doors if you allow it to open.

Just trust the process, and when things go wrong, don't let it change your focus.

Every team in the world is practicing, going over scouting reports, team matchups, and focusing on getting better. To separate yourself from the other players, you must put in the extra time away from the team.

During the separation, getting with a skill trainer three times a week, working with a strength coach twice a week, and getting with a parent or friend to help you up your game shots four days a week will increase your performance. A player must know his strong driving side on the court as well as his hot spot.

Chapter 6: Focus Points

What's your mindset when you're on the practice floor?

Do you look the coach in the eyes when he is speaking?

Do you focus during the entire practice?

Do you work to be at the front of the line each drill?

Do you show compassion to your teammates every practice?

Do you value the team and your role?

Are you disciplined on defense?

Do you foul out a lot?

Do you look to score?

Game Day

Game day is all about having a strong focus before the game. In middle school and high school, a player still has to attend classes, turn in homework, and continue his daily routine. Every break in the day, a player should think about the matchup and how he will impact the game.

During his lunch break, a player should speak with the coach or players about the game plan. Make sure your team captain is always ready to stay in a leadership role. Break down your assignments on both ends of the court.

First, know everything you are responsible for in the game and focus on your impact in helping the team become successful. Doing a walkthrough is key. This is the point where a player should see himself doing everything in the game. Focus on all the details, and send positive messages to the team and coaching staff. For example, telling the team, "great job, let's go harder," and on missed shots and plays, saying they will get the next one and "let's keep working."

In the locker room, 30 minutes before game time, get loose, get your blood flowing, and make sure teammates are on the same page. Have the captain reduce the horse playing until after the game, be committed, and go completely into game mode. Warm up at this point; the game is about to start soon. Make sure that you stretch well and that the team is talking to one another about responsibility and getting close.

Tip-Off

Be ready to make your impact on the game, and remember that being a good teammate is important. Players that often criticize are seldom forgiven; however, the player who encourages is seldom forgotten. Every player of the team has a role. Know what your role is and be effective in your approach and execution.

Give it your all, and after the game, let everyone know they did a good job. Win or lose, we will keep working on getting the next one.

Game Day Focus Points

Have you played the game in your mind the day before?

Do you get your muscles warmed up during pregame?

Do you have a clear understanding of defensive and offensive principles?

Can you focus on the match before the game starts?

Do you know the opposing team's best driver, shooter, rebounder, and defender?

Are you able to show mental toughness when needed?

Do you respect the game enough after a win or loss not to take a negative approach toward the next game?

Chapter 7

The Knowledge Tree

Words of Wisdom from Great Players

Sometimes the best teacher is the past experience of others. This section is built on knowledge taken from the journey of players that are where you want to be and come from where you are right now. Read their experiences and take the knowledge from their tree to help you become a better student-athlete.

Whitney Jones

University of Arkansas (Razorbacks)

Turkey, Italy, the Czech Republic, and Germany

What's the best part about playing at the college level?

The best part about playing at the collegiate level is facing different levels of competition.

What's the hardest part about playing at that level?

The challenges and growth on and off the court each year are difficult. The hardest part about playing at the collegiate level was injuries within the team and having to adjust and play out of position because of several injuries.

Give one word that sticks with you from the experience.

One word that describes my experience is determination.

Go into detail about the one word emotionally, mentally, and physically.

It takes a certain level of toughness and determination to compete at the collegiate level. You must keep up in the classroom and show up every day at practices and games.

Ryven "Trigger" Jackson

Talladega College Calgary Storm in Canada

What's the best part about playing at the college level?

The best part of competing is being able to play against the best player in the world at a high level. Not many players have an opportunity to compete in the D1 Championship. It's a blessing to be able to compete at that level.

What's the hardest part about playing at the college level?

The hardest part was maintaining focus at all times because you never know when it's your time to shine.

Give one word that sticks with you from the experience.

Hard work!

Go into detail about the one word emotionally, mentally, and physically.

Emotionally, hard work stuck with me because when I got out of high school and played college ball, it was hard work, whether on or off the court. Mentally, you must be focused no matter what; hard work is a mental thing. Physically, if you don't have that dog in you, then you will not make it. If you cry about everything, you will not make it!

"Every time I go up to the rim, it's an 'And 1' not a foul in my eyes." — Ryven Jackson

AJ Walton

Baylor University Alumni

Currently playing in Poland

What's the best part about playing at the college level?

The best part about playing at the college level is being around other talented guys and grinding and striving to make your dreams come true. Doing what you love and getting a free education is amazing.

What is the hardest part about playing at the college level?

The hardest thing about playing at the college level would probably be balancing school, practice, free time, and putting in extra hours of work daily.

Give one word that sticks with you from the experience.

Something that stuck with me is this, "Early is on time. On time, you are late."

Kim Adams Jr.

Arkansas State University/Overseas (Europe)

What's the best part about playing at the college level?

The best part about playing college ball for me was the game time, atmosphere, road trips, and playing in front of a big crowd on the road.

What's the hardest part about playing at the college level?

The hardest part is getting used to the grind, the early morning practices at 5, mandatory breakfast at 7, class at 8, evening practice around 3, and study hall later that night.

Give one word that sticks with you from the experience.

One word that sticks with me from my experience would be dedication.

Go into detail about the one word emotionally, mentally, and physically.

When it comes to being dedicated to the game of basketball emotionally, it's like a passion. You've got to love doing it to reap all the benefits that come with playing because it's a lot of hard work that you have to put into it behind the scenes when no one's looking. As far as mentally, you have to have a strong mind because there were so many times when I wanted to quit. One time, in particular, was my first year overseas in Portugal. I was far away from home. The food was different. Not too many people spoke English, and I had very little means of contacting my family and friends back home. One day, I broke down crying, saying I wanted to go home, but deep down inside, I knew I had to change my mindset because this is what I had dreamed of. All the hard work that I put into it and continued to put into it up to that point couldn't go to waste. So, from that point on, I became even stronger mentally, and I dedicated my game to trying to have a mental edge over other players whom I played against. Last but not least, being physically dedicated, with me being an undersized big man, I had to be physically dedicated to the game of basketball. If not, then I wouldn't have made it past high school. When I got to college, I weighed 195. The first few months were rough for me because I was playing against older guys. They were stronger than I was, but as I became dedicated to the weight room, I became stronger. By the time the season came, I was 220 with 7% body fat. From then on, there was no looking back. I knew I had to be dedicated to the game of basketball in all aspects for me to excel to the next level and for me to play at a high level. I was never the best player on any team as far as talent goes, but I was one of the top players, if not the top player on the team, as far as dedicating myself to the game of basketball.

Vincent Hunter Jr.

University of Arkansas/ 13-year pro

What's the best part about playing at the college level?

Creating lifelong friendships with people from all over the nation and playing in front of 50,000 plus fans every game.

What's the hardest part about playing at that level?

The physical conditioning that you must put your body through and being away from your family when things get tough.

Give one word that sticks with you from the experience.

Perseverance.

Go into detail about the one word emotionally, mentally, and physically.

Playing at a high level will test you emotionally, physically, and mentally. You can never be prepared for any of these challenges. You must learn as you go. Physically, you will have to push your body to the point of exhaustion. You will hurt. It will be painful. You will bleed. You will be sore, but in the end, it's worth it. Mentally, the game of basketball is played 85% to 90% in between your ears.

Tyler Scaife

Hall High School McDonald's All American

Rutgers University

Lebanon, China, Brazil, Germany

What's the best part about playing at the college level?

The best thing about playing at the collegiate level is being able to compete at a high level every day in practice. For me, this is how I look at life. Every day is a competition; you are either going to win the day or lose it.

What's the hardest part about playing at that level?

The hardest part about playing basketball at the college level is adjusting to all the travel, games, practices, lifts, and meetings while still balancing a social life.

Give one word that sticks with you from the experience.

One word that describes my experience is perseverance.

Go into detail about the one word emotionally, mentally, and physically.

Basketball is my love, but everything we do on the court translates into real life. Every day you will experience obstacles, and you will have to decide that you will overcome whatever is in your way. The mindset of never giving up and pushing through when things get hard is what will lead you to success not only on the court but also in everyday life. What happens in the time between where you are in life and where you want to be in life does not matter once your reach your goal.

Ricshanda Bickham

Nicholls State/McDonogh 35 and Pine High School

What's the best part about playing at the college level?

The best part about playing at the college level was getting my education paid for, leaving school with no student loan debt, competition, and meeting lifelong friends.

What's the hardest part about playing at that level?

The hardest part of playing in college is juggling school, athletics, and a social life, as well as long days like morning workouts, class, weights, study halls, and practices.

What's the difference between high school and college-level ball?

The level of competition is the main difference between high school and college. Another difference is your level of independence. In college, you don't have your parents there giving you that extra push.

Elaborate on the concept of working hard.
I always had basketball talent, and I learned at an early age that talent alone wouldn't get you far. So, I worked hard my entire basketball career. Working hard got me a

full scholarship. It also allowed me to continue my career overseas. Now, in my professional life, I continued to work hard and bring all my experience from sports into the real world. In the real world, you need teamwork, integrity, hard work, and dedication. I now have a promising career in finance.

"Hard work beats talent when talent doesn't work hard!"

Kameisha Johnson

Connors State College

UTSA

What's the best part about playing at the college level?

The relationships that you develop with your teammates and travel experiences.

What's the hardest part about playing at the level?

It's tough mentally, and you don't have any time to focus on academics as much as you want to.

Give one word that sticks with you from the experience.

Commitment.

Go into detail about the one word emotionally, mentally, and physically.

You must be emotionally and mentally committed to the sport because if you're not, you can get distracted easily. You must be physically committed to pushing your body to its max potential.

Taylor Mumphrey

Connors State College (07-09)

University of Memphis (09-11)

What's the difference between high school and college-level ball?
I would say the pace/speed, how quickly you are to be in shape, learning drills, and knowing all the plays in the playbook.
I was fortunate during my last two years in HS (Cedar Hill High, Cedar Hill, TX) to have a coach who ran practices like a college program, so I really only remember having two overwhelming college practices.

What's the best part about playing at the college level?

Free gear (lol). Honestly, it was the work ethic I developed in my efforts to be the best player I could be.

What's the hardest part about playing at the level?

Balancing athletics and schoolwork.

Give one word that sticks with you from the experience.

Perseverance.

Go into detail about the one word emotionally, mentally, and physically.

There were a lot of tough days in college on the court and off, but what kept me going was my end goal—graduating and not having my parents worried about paying for college. So, for all the early morning practices, long hours, road trips, study halls, and everything else that comes with being a student-athlete, I kept my mind on my end goal and persevered throughout the entire college athlete experience!

Terrell

Central Baptist College

Belize

What's the best part about playing at the college level?

The best part about playing at the college level is the level of competition you get to face and the travel.

What's the hardest part about playing at the level?

The hardest part about college basketball is when it's over (lol).

Give one word that sticks with you from the experience.

One word that stuck with me throughout college was "work."

Go into detail about the one word emotionally, mentally, and physically.

I was never the best player, so I felt like I had to work 10x harder than everybody else just to keep up.

"Put your head down, go to work, and don't stop until you reach your goals." — T||T Elite

Anonymous

ESPN Top 50 player/ACC

What's the difference between high school and college-level ball?

The biggest difference between middle school, high school, and college is the competition level. Most of the time, as you get older, the competition level starts to rise. Next is how serious the players took that game. Some did it as a hobby, and some wanted to play college basketball. Coaches wanted those who were serious about basketball as well. Third, college differs from both middle and high school in the sense that basketball becomes a priority, especially if you're on a scholarship. They can take that scholarship away just as quickly as they gave it to you. College can be hard, or it can be tolerable. If you start to prep and get used to working hard at a young age, then it becomes second nature, and it's easy because you've been working hard from day one.

What's the best part about playing at the college level?

The best part about being a college athlete is being able to compete against some of the best players around the world. I love competition. I want to be challenged and to play against the best. Winning against the best makes the win feel even better.

What's the hardest part about playing at the college level?

The hardest part is that you're not a normal student in college. You're a student-athlete. With that being said, while you work hard on the court, you must work just as hard off the court. It's easier said than done. You may struggle at some point, but if you stay focused, it will get easier.

Give one word that sticks with you from the experience.

Persistence.

Go into detail about the one word emotionally, mentally, and physically.

It's inevitable that while playing in college, you are going to face adversity mentally and physically, but it's how you respond to said adversity that will make you or break you. However, being persistent in achieving success is what helped me.

In middle school, I gained my confidence because I always felt like I was the best player on the floor. From middle school to high school, I learned to be more vocal. When I was younger, I was a lead-by-example type of person, but my coach told me that my voice was just as important as my actions. Plus, I was a point guard, so it was a must that I became vocal. From high school to college, I gained maturity. By that I mean I adjusted how I responded to criticism. I stayed coachable, and I put the team's success first.

Shekinna Stricklen

University of Tennessee

Mc Donald's All American, 2nd pick in WNBA Draft/ Current team Atlanta Dream

What's the best part about playing at the college level?

Playing in front of thousands of fans!

What's the hardest part about playing at that level?

The hardest part is the training and balancing school work. I was so determined to be the best I could be in college! The workouts were very tough, and I was determined to push myself! I was determined to graduate and put myself in the best possible position to get drafted!

Nyeshia Stevenson

Gatorade Athlete of the year

University of Oklahoma/ Big 12's Sixth Man award with 2 back to back final 4 Appearance
36 pick in WNBA Draft by Phoenix Mercury
Team Parma (Italy)
Team Habikaa (Israel)

What's the best part about playing at the college level?

The best part about playing at the college level is the amount of growth your game can elevate if you apply yourself.

What's the hardest part about playing at that level?

The hardest part is being able to balance both school and ball. Not saying it can't be done. Just saying it can get hectic, and it's easy to fall behind and have to play catch-up.

Give one word that sticks with you from the experience.

One word that sticks with me from my experience is GRIT.

Go into detail about the one word emotionally, mentally, and physically.

Grit simply means passion and perseverance for long-term

and meaningful goals. It is the ability to persist in something you feel passionate about and persevere when you face obstacles. This kind of passion is not about intense emotions or infatuation.

Nakeia Guiden

University is Central Arkansas / 1000-point club

What's the best part about playing at the college level?
Playing against the top talent and seeing how I could hold my own while playing with some great teammates.

What's the hardest part about playing at that level?
Balancing classwork while traveling for games.

Give one word that sticks with you from the experience.

Perseverance.

Go into detail about the one word emotionally, mentally, and physically.

Playing at the college level was the biggest challenge I've ever encountered, from countless 5 am workouts to only playing the last 2 minutes of the Tulsa game my freshman year after being a starter/all-star in high school.

Those experiences really tested my patience and love for the game. I felt the Lord blessed me with an opportunity to prove myself, and I did just that.

I earned a starting spot as well as a spot in UCA's 1,000+ points club. From that point on, perseverance was my best

friend, and I wouldn't change it for anything.

Tiffany Davis

High School - Carson High School / Cerritos College
Professional team - Long Beach Sharks (WSPBL)

What's the best part about playing at the college level?

In high school, you will play against top talent every now and then, but college ball is the best of the best.

What's the hardest part about playing at the level?

Being a team player. At every level of basketball, I was challenged to utilize the system. I was super competitive, and I just wanted to get it done myself—on both ends of the floor.

Give one word that sticks with you from the experience

Discipline.

Go into detail about the one word, emotionally, mentally, and physically.

Playing basketball forced me to develop strong discipline emotionally, mentally, and physically. I am a true-to-heart competitor. I hate losing. Losing would stir up so many emotions. I had to learn to be emotionally disciplined to use those emotions to drive me to better. My mental discipline was also forced. I had to learn how to block outside distractions during practice and game times. My mental focus was a game-changer. I was always physically disciplined. I wanted to be the fastest, the strongest, and jump the highest. I liked being able to hold my own as a guard mixing it up with the bigs. I enjoyed being the player other teams practiced for. My favorite moment in my career was hearing the opposing coach yell, "Who's got, Tiffany? 15! 15! Who's got 15!"

How can sports help you transition into life as an adult?
Playing team sports taught me to depend on others in a team setting. I learned to focus and use my talents, and the discipline to be the best and always give my all has helped me be a successful employee and business owner.

Chapter 7: Focus Points

What did you learn from the players?

How can you apply their knowledge to help fit your skillset?

What is the mindset of a player working to be great?

What is the difference between a great player and an average player?

How important are your grades?

How do you apply lessons learned from basketball to your life?

Are you a good listener?

Do you set goals?

Nyeshia "Ny" Stevenson

Nyeshia "Ny" Stevenson with Hall of Fame Coach Charles Ripley.

National Signing Day for Nyeshia "Ny" Stevenson, ready to head to the University of Oklahoma.

National Signing Day for Marlesha Piggee for the University of Central Arkansas.

National Signing Day for Mike Hawkins, who signed with Shawnee Community College with Head Coach John Sparks.

University of Arkansas' Vincent Hunter

Vincent Hunter

University of Arkansas' Whitney Jones

Whitney Jones: A Focused Shooter

Connor State Women Basketball:
Ready for the Big Stage

Chapter 8

Building A Positive Support System

Wisdom from Parents, Coaches, and Trainers.

To have success in the game of basketball, it is vital to have a strong support system. Your support system may consist of your parents, teachers, coaches, friends, and so on. Your biggest fans 90% of the time will be your parents. Your parents invest in your dreams, allow you to grow, and are always the ones there on the ground level in most cases.

Coaches can consist of the head of the organization, the head basketball coach, the strength and conditioning coach, and the player development coach. They are the ones who support the development of your skills and put you in different situations to promote your growth.

Below are some comments from parents' experiences in the development of their children.

There are also key pointers from strength and conditioning coaches and player development coaches designed to help increase athletic performance.

Parents of 2020 Mc Donald's All-American

Rank Top 20 in 2020 Class

IMG Academy

When did you know your child had the talent to play the sport?

We noticed around age 9.

At what age was your child at the top of his/her class or his/her game?

He was around 11 years old.

What's the difference between high school and college?

There is no difference between high school and college; we keep our circle small.

Was it hard to support your child at games and work also?

No, it wasn't hard to support my child and work. I was blessed to have a job I've been on for many years that allowed me the flexibility to travel.

Did your child play college ball in-state or out-of-state?

My son will be playing college basketball out-of-state at the

University of Tennessee.

Was this a hard experience?

This was a great experience!

What did you learn from the experience?

I've learned it takes sacrifice, dedication, hard work, and patience.

What is the best information learned from the experience?

The information learned from this experience is that if your child works hard and stays focused, he can achieve his dreams.

Datron and MeLesha Humphrey

Archie Goodwin

Sylvan Hills High School/ University of KY

When did you know your child had the talent to play the sport?

In the beginning, we were just giving him something recreational to do. I noticed the talent between the ages of 8 and 10.

At what age was your child at the top of his class/his game?

10th grade.

What's the difference between middle school and high school from a support point of view?

The support has pretty much always been the same on all platforms.

What's the difference between high school and college?

The traveling to high school games was a lot easier, which made it possible to be at all his games. College games would have required further distances making it harder to see him play outside of televised games.

Was it hard to support your child at games and work also?

It was a challenge, but we made it happen.

Did your child play college ball in-state or out-of-state?

Out-of-state.

Was this a hard experience? If so, why?

The hardest part was not being able to see him due to the distance.

What is the best information you have learned from the experience?

All things are possible when you put in the work and have a dependable, supportive cast.

Anonymous Parents

Freshman Student

Parkview

When did you know your child had the talent to play the sport?

At first, she played because she liked to play at 3. Then, as she grew older, she was overweight for her height. She was off the growth chart, and as she played, she fell in love with the game at the age of 11!

At what age was your child at the top of her class or her game?

11.

What's the difference between middle school and high school from a support point of view?

Full support.

What's the difference between high school and college?

There's no difference. She will receive full support.

Was it hard to support your child at games and work also?

No.

Did your child play college ball in-state or out-of-state?

She is in the 10th grade.

Was this a hard experience? If so, why?

No.

What did you learn from the experience?

We're still learning.

What is the best information you have learned from the experience?

Always be willing to give it your all during every practice and game.

Stacey and Yvonne Stevenson

Nyeshia Stevenson

McClellan Magnet High School/University of Oklahoma

When did you know your child had the talent to play the sport?

We knew that Nyeshia had the talent to play the sport when she was in the 6th grade at Pulaski Heights Middle School.

At what age was your child at the top of her class or her game?

Ny was at the top of her game at the age of 13 in her 8th-grade year and continued to improve in her high-school tenure as well as her college experience.

What's the difference between middle school and high school from a support point of view?

In our experience, the support at the middle-school level was great because you had more parents in the stands as well as working in the concession so that they could be a presence in the lives of their students/athletes. In high school, you had the presence of parents but not in as vast of an amount as the middle school forum. I think that, as parents, we assume that our children do not need our support as much in high school, but we have to understand that they are going to be transitioning into adulthood. They will need our support even more.

What's the difference between high school and college?

There is a huge difference in support between high school versus support in college. In high school, you have the presence of some parents in the stands and the option to speak with the coaches about your child's progress in the classroom and on and off the court. At the college level, you support from the stands or the audience at the end of the year banquet. Now, I was that parent who spoke with the college coaches about the progress of Ny on the court and in the classroom. When you speak with any coach on any level, there needs to be a level of respect for your approach and not a demanding attitude on why your child or athlete should be playing. The coaches or anyone else will not receive it well.

Was it hard to support your child at games and work also?

It was not hard to support Ny while working because Stacey and I had careers that afforded us the opportunity to be at her games. Our supervisors were always supportive and understanding if we had to leave early for an out-of-town game. That was truly a blessing.

Did your child play college ball in-state or out-of-state?

Nyeshia played basketball out-of-state at the University of Oklahoma located in Norman, OK. The experience was hard in the beginning because we were used to attending all of Ny's games. It got better when we could watch the televised games and the online games so that we could continue to see her flourish in the game. It was always exciting to watch her in person and on television. Stacey and I learned that we had to give up the opportunity to attend all of her games so that she could grow into adulthood without always being dependent on us to experience different life experiences and to transition into adulthood, knowing that she had our support when needed.

What is the best information you have learned from the experience?

The best information that we learned from the experience is that there are many opportunities waiting for your student/athlete. As parents, it is our responsibility to prepare them as much as possible by giving them support in the classroom, on the court, and through their teenage experiences. We must help them improve their testing skills as well as their communication and speaking skills.

Anthony and Loretta Walton

Anthony Walton, Jr. "AJ Walton"

Hall High School/Baylor University

When did you know your child had the talent to play the sport?

When AJ was in the 2nd grade, he was 8 years old.

At what age was your child at the top of his class or his game?

Age 14, eighth grade.

What's the difference between middle school and high school from a support point of view?

The student starts to take the sport more seriously and looks for a future with the game.

What's the difference between high school and college-level ball?

The level of play is more intense, competition is greater, and there are better players to compete against.

Was it hard to support your child at games and work also?

No, because we have always told our children that you do what you have to early in life so that you can do what you want to later in life when you need to do it. We didn't miss games because our children were always looking for us to be there.

Did your child play college ball in-state or out-of-state?

Out-of-state, and that was best because he didn't have his high-school buddies around to distract him, and if he got into trouble, we didn't know about it. We threatened him that if he went to Baylor and embarrassed our name, he would have to come home.

Was this a hard experience? If so, why?

Sometimes, seeing college coaches play favoritism was heartbreaking. We were honest parents and always taught our children to be that way. We always put God first, and we had a good supportive church family and friends.

What did you learn from the experience?

Parents should encourage their children to be the best they can be, to have a good support system, to be honest, and to treat people the way they want to be treated always.

What is the best information you have learned from the experience?

Teach your child to be humble, and God will send good coaches such as yourself, Coach Clark, to guide them. I do believe the Universe used you, Coach Clark, to help AJ because you tookhim to his first Baylor visit. We really had never thought of Baylor as a possible college for AJ, and for that, we will always

Strength Coach Whitney Jones

Fit with Whit

Tips For Getting Fit

Building Upper/Lower Body Strength

The best way to build upper/lower body strength is by challenging yourself in the weight room! Strength and conditioning are crucial for on-court performance. Challenge your body every session in the weight room!

Focus on Schoolwork and Develop Fundamentals

A middle-school athlete should focus on schoolwork first and foremost and developing fundamentals. Gaining knowledge of the game on both sides of the ball is important.

The Importance of Nutrition

Nutrition in middle school and high school is very important! The sooner you learn the benefits of nutrition and how it can improve performance on the court, the better. If you start young, then, by the time you get to college, it won't be such a rude awakening or a hard adjustment. You may be able to get away with eating unhealthy when you're younger, but once you get to college and are older, it's a necessity. It's the little things you do off the court that separate you from other athletes (weight room, nutrition, etc.). There's no way around it.

Be Coachable

A kid can keep from stunting his growth in middle school by being coachable/teachable. You always have to be willing to listen and learn.

Avoid Excess

A person can definitely over lift. Too much of anything is bad for you. Lift enough to where your body is under stress but not too much stress to where it causes joint pain. If it's so heavy that you're not able to use proper form while lifting, drop down and work your way up to heavier weights down the line. Improper lifting leads to injuries on the court. Learn to listen to your body!

Your Core

Basketball muscles, your core (hip flexors, abs, and back muscles), this is your body's foundation. Shoulder muscles, triceps, biceps, and forearm muscles are important for shooting. Quads, hams, and calves are important for jumping/quickness.

High-School Workout

In high school, you should work out at least 5-6 days per week. Allow yourself at least one day per week to rest and recover when needed. I was in the gym or was doing some type of work just about every day, including Sundays.

Weightlifting

You should lift weights during the season because you need to maintain the muscle that you built during the pre/offseason. During the season, you're only lifting to maintain, so this means that you shouldn't lift as heavy, hard, or as often as you do in the pre-season or off-season. You must keep those muscles built so that they can protect your joints/ligaments from injuries and provide your body with power when competing.

PROPER WEIGHTLIFTING WILL IMPROVE A PLAYER'S JUMP SHOT

Workouts

The best workout to do in pre/off-season is to condition, condition, and condition, i.e., prints, change of speed/direction, and long runs (1-3 miles). Individual workouts, as well as perfecting weaknesses on the court and in the weight room, are effective.

Chris Davis

Dawg House Basketball Skill Training LLC

How do you improve a client's skills?

We improve client's skillsets in many ways. We work on a lot of details and small underlying nuance skills that are mostly overlooked. The main part is that we meet every client where they are and build from there with a planned out progressive plan. Every workout is tracked and logged.

What's the first thing you look for when you're evaluating a new client?

When evaluating a new client, the first thing I look for is the willingness to work; that's all that matters to me. I couldn't care less about initial skill sets (if the player is good or not). We only allow players who are committed fully to expand their game and become better people in life.

How does a player improve his confidence level?
I feel that players improve their confidence levels by working hard to improve their skill sets. If you know you are working as hard as you can in the gym, that fact itself makes you believe in yourself while in the game because you know you

have prepared yourself properly.

What's the best way for a client to improve his shooting?
For clients to improve their shooting, many things come into play. The correct method to be used depends on the client's mechanical issues. Every client is different, so there's not one thing I'll say that fits every situation. After I see a player shoot, I record it, dissect it, and make a plan to get to a final, smooth, consistent technique.

How does your client take his workout to an organized gameplay setting?
Game translation is the truth of a trainer's methods. Everything we do is about bettering performance in-game. I ensure every session is 10x harder than what the game will be. I give detailed explanations as to why movements are made thoroughly so that my client fully understands specific reads. I simulate those reads many times throughout sessions to give the best possible chance of the client understanding game flow and openings in-game.

Player Development and Skills Training

Juwan Brown

Skills Distancing Club

How do you improve a client's skills?
I help improve client's skills through game-like skill work, working on the things that will happen the most in the game, and the counters to those things. Every player I work with has a strategic plan on what we need to improve to go to the next level. Most of my players are only working on 2-3 things all summer. Things are translated into your game through REPS.

What's the first thing you look for when you're evaluating a new client?
Their skill level at that moment (ball handling, footwork, shooting, and decision-making).

How does a player improve his confidence level?
Through consistent hard work on the things he will use in the game; confidence comes from the work you put in. Also, putting players in those uncomfortable situations in workouts is important, so once it's time for the game, it's not their first time being in that situation.

What's the best way for a client to improve his shooting?

Through consistent reps and consistent, correct form.

Tips for focusing a player's balance:

1. *Your Feet*
    a. Everyone's balance will be different because it's about what's comfortable to the shooter and where his feet would be if he did a standstill vertical jumper.
2. *Elbow*
    a. Elbow under the ball is a crucial thing.
3. *Eyes*
    a. Eyes on your target. Different players have different things they look at when shooting.
4. *Follow Through*
    a. Everything should be straight to the rim and the snap of the wrist with your fingers pointing down.

How does your client take his workout to an organized gameplay setting?

By having confidence in the things we've worked on and trusting the process he's been through when no one else was watching.

Chapter 8: Focus Points

Identify your biggest fans.

Are you willing to see a strength/player development coach 3 times a week?

What are 3 reasons it is important to have a support system?

Why should you value your parents?

How can a strength/player development coach increase your performance?

Why should you be proactive in basketball and life?

Are you willing to pay the price for success, extra time in practice, or working out at home by yourself or with a coach?

Do you have the potential to be a leader?

When no one is watching,
that's when your workouts count the most!

Chapter 9

Ranking and Playing on a National Level

Let me start by saying congratulations if you have made it this far in your basketball career. This means you have put in the work at the local level and now you are ready to see what skills it takes to play at a higher level.

The top places to test your skills are at exposure events, elite camps on the college campus and showcases, just to name a few.

The goal, when playing at this type of event, is to leave your mark! You want to leave a lasting impression with any sportswriters and event directors so that they remember your name. Make sure they know who you are after every performance.

Sometimes, it may take you walking right up to them and asking, "What do you think of my performance, and is there anything you feel that I can work on to improve my game?"

Most of the time, they will be right on. Always make a mental note, remember what they said, and see if it can help improve your basketball skills or lifestyle.

Always go after the top player at the camp, and if you are the top player, just know players are coming to take your spot.

Always network! You never know, as you age, which state you will be back in or where you will need to build a relationship for basketball. Always show respect for the game and the people in it. Have respect for the people who come to support you, and never get so big that you lose track of where you come from.

The grind, plan your summer, save your money for the summer, and do three big-time events. There's always someone watching, so make the best of it.

Note: Some of the top, middle- and high-school players have made their marks on the sport at the events listed below, which have helped pave the way to national rankings and a shot at becoming a High-School All-American.

Top Summer Camps
- U.S.A
- Point Guard College
- Advantage Basketball Camp
- Jason Otter School of Basketball
- Five Star Basketball
- NBC Basketball

- The Hoop Group

Showcases & Exposure Events (Middle School)
- Chris Paul All American Camp
- Pangos All American
- NEO Ohio

Top 100 Middle-School Showcase (North Carolina)
- Born to Hoop Camp in Arkansas
- National Camp Series-Hardwood Super 60

High-School Basketball Tournaments
- Battle in the Bluff
- Battle of the Apple
- Charlotte Hoops Challenge
- Gate City Classic
- King of the Bluegrass
- Rumble of the Ridge

The Court House

"The laws of what it takes to be a High-School All-American"

Bobby Bates (Co-Founder of the Iverson Classic or Allen Iverson Roundball Classic)

Law 1

You must be willing to put in the work to be the best on the court at all times.

Be able to stand out with your communication skills, look at the coach when he talks, and speak positively to your teammates by picking them up when they are down.

Law 2

You must be the player who wants it more than any other player in the world.

Don't let your parents be more passionate about your success than you.

Law 3

You must love the hard work that goes into the sport.

Know what drives you to want more out of the sport and life.

Law 4

Basketball is 90 percent mental and 10 percent physical. With the right mental toughness, the physical parts of the game become easy to manage.

It doesn't matter how you start; what matters is how you finish. Get better every day.

Law 5

Know the history of the sport, then study other great players. Know what made Kobe, Jordan, and Larry Bird special.

The blueprint has been created. Will you trust the process or talk about doing it without taking action?

Law 6

Don't play the game for likes on the internet. Put your time into your game (500 shots a day), and strengthen your game by playing older people who can push you to be better.

Players must stay humble and understand that somebody

helped them get to where they are today—parent, teacher, and mentor.

Key points

- Don't fake it halfway with one foot on the court and one foot off the court. Give it 100 percent and go all in.
- Don't say you want to be great like Kobe or LeBron when you're not willing to put in the work.
- All players should play the game daily, study the game film tape, and know the sport's history to try to become a High-School All-American.

Top High-School All-American Events

- Top High-School All-American Events
- McDonald's
- Iverson Classic or Allen Iverson Roundball Classic
- Jordan Brand
- Nike Hoop Summit
- NBA Top 100
- U.S.A.

Chapter 9: Focus Points

What does it take to be ranked?

How much work do you have to put in to be one of the top players in the nation?

What is one of the key laws given by Bobby Bates?

What should your personal drive be at an elite camp?

Are you willing to know the history of the sport?

Why is this important?

Bobby Bates and Allen Iverson, co-founders of the Iverson Classic or Allen Iverson Roundball Classic.

Archie Goodwin is focused and ready for the
McDonald's All-American Game.

Archie Goodwin working out before the Jordan Brand Classic Game.

Here is Crystal Boyd giving an all-star performance at the McDonald's All-American game.

Chapter 10

Set Your Table

Start thinking about the information below. This will help you find focus. Use it as a roadmap toward making a mark on your athletic journey.

Name

_____

Sport

_____

Years of experience _____

Position

_____

Who do you study?

_____

What's your personal goal?

_____

How often do you watch basketball on video?

_____

What's is the highest level at which you dream of playing?

_____

Do you compete and work hard every time you hit the court?

_____

Do you have a faithful support system?

_____

Do you network with the people who play this sport?

_____

Do you respect the people who have helped you learn the sport?

_____

Do you understand your life purpose? _____

What is recruiting?

_____

_____

How many schools can recruit you at one time?

_____

How do middle-school and high-school coaches impact your development?

_____

_____

Do you have a mentor?

_____

What knowledge can you pass down from parent(s) and mentor(s) who have impacted you?

_____

_____

What life lessons have made you a stronger person?

_____

_____

Are you a team player?

_____

Chapter 10: Focus Points

What is your daily workout plan?

What are 10 positive words you use daily?

Are you willing to help around the house and keep your box (bedroom, locker room, backpack, desk, car, etc.) in order?

Question:

How Do You Make a Difference in Your Community?

Answer:

Always be willing to give back.

Daily Journal

Use the next few pages to begin journaling about the process of how to level up your goals, your focus, and your attention. Do you understand the process of leveling up? Do you make the connection between sports goals and life goals? Use these pages to mark your success!

Daily Journal

Daily Journal

Daily Journal

Daily Journal

Daily Journal

Daily Journal

Daily Journal

Daily Journal

Daily Journal

Daily Journal

Daily Journal

Daily Journal

Daily Journal

Daily Journal

Daily Journal

Daily Journal

Daily Journal

Daily Journal

# Daily Journal

Daily Journal

Daily Journal

Daily Journal

Daily Journal

Daily Journal

Daily Journal

Daily Journal

Daily Journal

Daily Journal

Daily Journal

Daily Journal

Daily Journal

Daily Journal

Daily Journal

Daily Journal

Daily Journal

Daily Journal

Daily Journal

Daily Journal

Daily Journal

Daily Journal

Always be willing to give it your all.

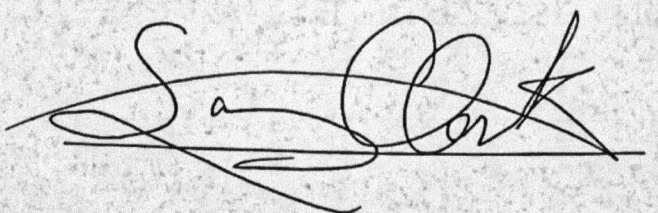

Sammy Clark

Author

About the Author

Sammy Clark holds a bachelor's degree in Health Sciences and a master's in Adult Education from the University of Arkansas, Little Rock. Coach Clark also has more than twenty years of experience in all levels of coaching. Among his accomplishments include developing NBA players Archie Goodwin and Darryl Macon, as well as other NBA/WNBA and collegiate players.

As an Arkansas difference-maker, Sammy Clark has taken on the challenge of empowering the youth of tomorrow through mentorship and leadership counseling.

Clark is a loving and caring person. He is also the proud father of Samuel Clark, who is a class of 2021 senior.

Champions are built from within.

Scott Drew (signature)

Scott Drew, Head Coach

Baylor University

Come into every practice with the will to win the day.

[signature] Phil 4:13

Johnnie Harris, Head Coach

University of Auburn

Versatility is something that stands out.

[signature]

Eric Musselman, Head Coach

University of Arkansas

We Make Good Great!

www.butterflytypeface.com

www.ingramcontent.com/pod-product-compliance
Lightning Source LLC
LaVergne TN
LVHW012210070526
838202LV00032B/2647/J